MW01225815

Literacy Consultants
DAVID BOOTH • KATHLEEN GOULD LUNDY

Social Studies Consultant
PETER PAPPAS

A Harcourt Achieve Imprint

10801 N. Mopac Expressway
Building # 3
Austin, TX 78759
1.800.531.5015

Steck-Vaughn is a trademark of Harcourt Achieve Inc. registered in the United States of America and/or other jurisdictions. All inquiries should be mailed to: Paralegal Department, 6277 Sea Harbor Drive, Orlando, FL 32887.

 © 2007 Rubicon Publishing Inc.
www. rubiconpublishing.com

Project Editor: Kim Koh
Editor: Vicki Low
Art Director: Jen Harvey
Project Designer: Jan-John Rivera

7 8 9 10 11   5 4 3 2 1

Napoleon's Last Stand
ISBN 13: 978-1-4190-3208-0
ISBN 10:   1-4190-3208-9

Printed in Singapore

PHOTO CREDITS: istockphoto: 2-5, 13, 21, 29, 37, 45-47; The Granger Collection, New York: 4, 13, 21, 29, 37, 45-47

NAPOLEON'S LAST STAND

Written by

DAVID BOYD

Illustrated by

DAVID OKUM

NAPOLEON BONAPARTE

DUKE OF WELLINGTON

CHARLOTTE

LUCIEN

FREDERICK

REAL PEOPLE IN HISTORY

NAPOLEON BONAPARTE (1769–1821): A French general who became Emperor of France.

DUKE OF WELLINGTON (1769–1852): The English general who defeated Napoleon at Waterloo. He was also called the "Iron Duke."

CHARLOTTE BONAPARTE (1802–1839): Napoleon's niece who moved to America after Napoleon's defeat at Waterloo.

FICTIONAL CHARACTERS

LUCIEN: Charlotte Bonaparte's eight-year-old son.

FREDERICK: A French officer who helps Charlotte after the Battle of Waterloo.

Contents

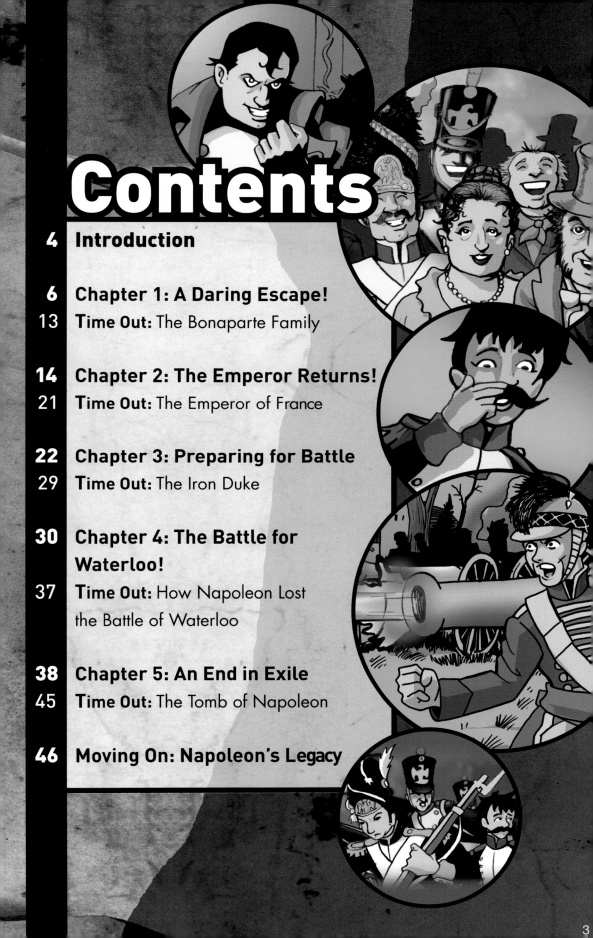

Napoleon
Bonaparte

Napoleon Bonaparte was an outstanding military figure. He took part in the French Revolution. This was a time when the French people overthrew the monarchy and formed a new government.

1769	1793	1796	1799
Napoleon Bonaparte is born on the island of Corsica.	Napoleon is made general during the French Revolution.	Napoleon becomes commander of the French Army of Italy.	Napoleon helps to overthrow the government of the First Republic in Paris.

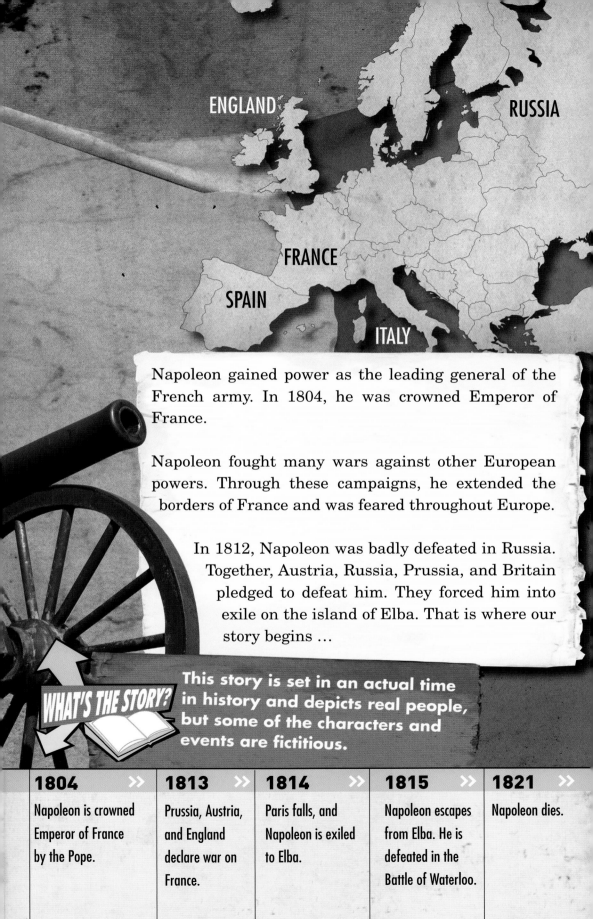

ENGLAND

RUSSIA

FRANCE

SPAIN

ITALY

Napoleon gained power as the leading general of the French army. In 1804, he was crowned Emperor of France.

Napoleon fought many wars against other European powers. Through these campaigns, he extended the borders of France and was feared throughout Europe.

In 1812, Napoleon was badly defeated in Russia. Together, Austria, Russia, Prussia, and Britain pledged to defeat him. They forced him into exile on the island of Elba. That is where our story begins …

WHAT'S THE STORY? This story is set in an actual time in history and depicts real people, but some of the characters and events are fictitious.

1804 »	1813 »	1814 »	1815 »	1821 »
Napoleon is crowned Emperor of France by the Pope.	Prussia, Austria, and England declare war on France.	Paris falls, and Napoleon is exiled to Elba.	Napoleon escapes from Elba. He is defeated in the Battle of Waterloo.	Napoleon dies.

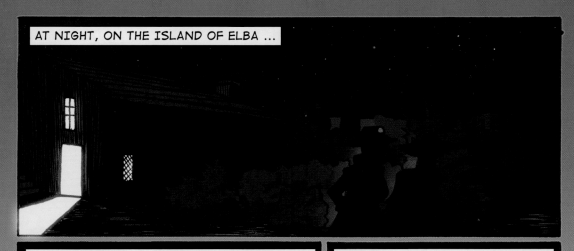

AT NIGHT, ON THE ISLAND OF ELBA ...

TWO ENGLISH GUARDS WATCH AND FOLLOW AS BONAPARTE AND HIS NIECE WALK TOWARD THE SMALL HARBOR.

AS LONG AS NAPOLEON DOESN'T GET INTO THE SMALL BOAT WITH HIS NIECE, ALL IS WELL.

AS THE BOAT LEAVES WITHOUT NAPOLEON, THE GUARDS RELAX.

BUT THE NEXT MORNING, TWO DIFFERENT GUARDS ESCORT CHARLOTTE BONAPARTE DOWN TO THE HARBOR AGAIN! DIDN'T SHE LEAVE ELBA THE NIGHT BEFORE?

NAPOLEON'S ESCAPE IS SOON DISCOVERED.

WE CAN'T FIND HIM ANYWHERE! HE'S ESCAPED!

THAT'S IMPOSSIBLE!

CHARLOTTE LAUGHS AS SHE RECALLS NAPOLEON'S ESCAPE.

HAHA! YOU STILL HAVE THE HAT, DON'T YOU, MAMA?

YES, I DO. NAPOLEON LOOKED SO SILLY IN THAT DRESS AND MY HAT! THE DRESS WAS WHAT MY PACKAGE CONTAINED!

AND BECAUSE HE WAS A LITTLE MAN, HE LOOKED FROM A DISTANCE ON A DARK NIGHT ...

JUST LIKE HIS 13-YEAR-OLD NIECE!

THE BONAPARTE FAMILY

Joseph Bonaparte

Napoleon was born on the island of Corsica, off the coast of Italy. Corsica was, and still is, a French territory, but its people are more closely related to the Italians than to the French. Napoleon's father was a lawyer who supported the French control of Corsica. As a result, Napoleon and his brother Joseph were allowed to study at the finest French military schools and colleges.

Napoleon had three sisters and four brothers. When he became Emperor of France, he gave them royal titles, land, and money. His brother Joseph was made King of Spain.

Napoleon did have a niece named Charlotte. She was Joseph's daughter. She held the titles Princess of France and Infanta (daughter of the King) of Spain.

SPAIN

After Napoleon's defeat at the Battle of Waterloo, Joseph fled to Switzerland before going to America. He settled in Point Breeze, New Jersey. Charlotte moved back to Europe after a few years and settled in Italy.

A MILE ALONG THE ROAD, THEY MEET WITH ARMED TROOPS! NEWS OF NAPOLEON'S ESCAPE HAS SPREAD.

DON'T MOVE! I SHALL SPEAK WITH THEM!

BROTHERS! IF YOU WISH TO STRIKE YOUR EMPEROR DOWN, DO SO NOW!

I AM ON MY WAY TO PARIS TO RECLAIM MY THRONE. I WILL RAISE THE GLORY OF FRANCE TO NEW HEIGHTS!

KILL ME HERE OR JOIN ME ON MY GLORIOUS CAMPAIGN!

THE SOLDIERS CHEER LOUDLY! NAPOLEON BONAPARTE IS BACK!

HURRAY!

FOR TWO WEEKS, NAPOLEON TRAVELS TOWARD PARIS. THE PEOPLE FLOCK TO HIS BANNER.

NAPOLEON HAS ESCAPED! HE IS ON THE RISE AGAIN!

IN ENGLAND AND THE REST OF EUROPE, HOWEVER, PEOPLE PANIC AT THE NEWS OF NAPOLEON'S RETURN.

OH! THE IRON DUKE MUST SAVE US FROM NAPOLEON!

GATHER MY ARMIES! WE'LL TEACH NAPOLEON A LESSON HE'LL NEVER FORGET!

ON THE DAY OF NAPOLEON'S RETURN TO PARIS, THOUSANDS OF CITIZENS AND SOLDIERS LINE THE FAMOUS CHAMPS-ELYSÉES TO SEE THEIR EMPEROR PASS BY!

NAPOLEON'S GENERALS FOLLOW, SUPPORTED BY THEIR TROOPS.

GENERAL, SEE HOW THE PEOPLE LOVE ME!

THEY HAVE BEEN WAITING FOR YOUR RETURN, MY EMPEROR! WHAT A GLORIOUS DAY FOR FRANCE!

I HAVE WORD FROM OUR SPIES THAT WELLINGTON IS ON THE MOVE AGAINST US.

LET HIM COME, EMPEROR! NO ARMY OF FRANCE CAN BE DEFEATED WHEN YOU ARE LEADING IT.

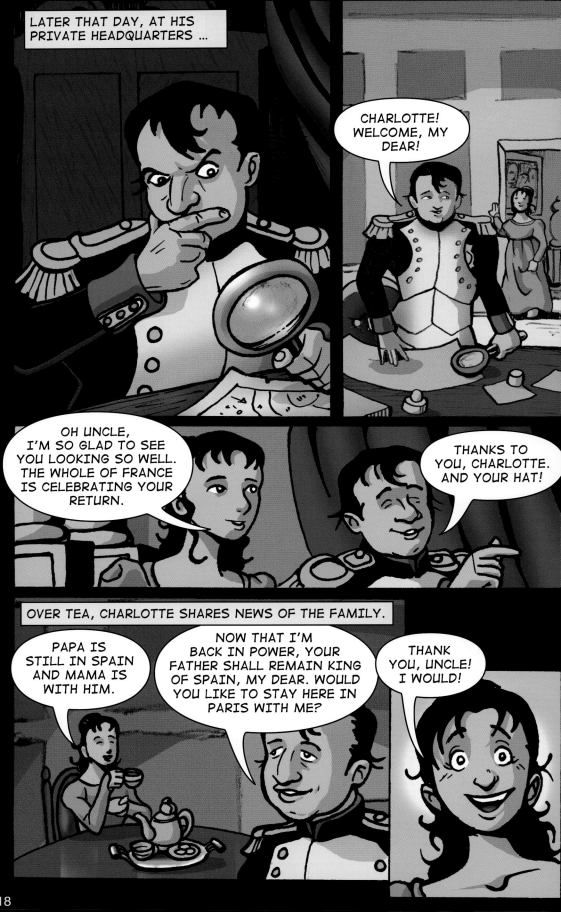

WITH HER MAIDS' HELP, CHARLOTTE UNPACKS HER SUITCASE.

THERE'S SOMETHING SPECIAL HERE THAT I DON'T WANT TO HAVE WRINKLED!

IT BELONGED TO MY UNCLE JEROME WHEN HE WAS A JUNIOR OFFICER. IT'S A PERFECT FIT FOR ME!

MADAME MEANS TO WEAR THIS UNIFORM?

I MOST CERTAINLY DO! NOW, SOPHIE, YOU MUST CUT MY HAIR SHORT.

Napoleon Bonaparte
as Emperor of France

THE EMPEROR OF FRANCE

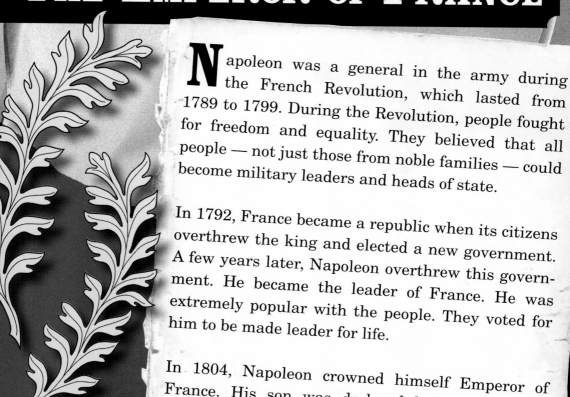

Napoleon was a general in the army during the French Revolution, which lasted from 1789 to 1799. During the Revolution, people fought for freedom and equality. They believed that all people — not just those from noble families — could become military leaders and heads of state.

In 1792, France became a republic when its citizens overthrew the king and elected a new government. A few years later, Napoleon overthrew this government. He became the leader of France. He was extremely popular with the people. They voted for him to be made leader for life.

In 1804, Napoleon crowned himself Emperor of France. His son was declared heir to his title. So even though he had fought to overthrow the monarchy, Napoleon in effect brought it back.

IN THE MIDDLE OF THE NIGHT, WELLINGTON GATHERS HIS GENERALS.

OLD BONEY HAS CLOSE TO 100,000 TROOPS IN THE FIELD. TOGETHER WITH OUR BELGIAN AND DUTCH ALLIES, WE STAND AT 70,000.

AND OUR PRUSSIAN FRIEND BLUCHER HAS GATHERED 110,000 TROOPS.

MORE THAN ENOUGH TO DEFEAT OLD BONEY, I RECKON!

PERHAPS. NUMBERS DO NOT ALWAYS TELL THE TALE, MY FRIEND. OTHERWISE, WHAT WOULD WE COMMANDERS HAVE TO DO? HA! HA!

YES, WE HAVE MORE MEN THAN NAPOLEON, BUT BLUCHER'S TROOPS ARE A HALF A DAY'S MARCH AWAY.

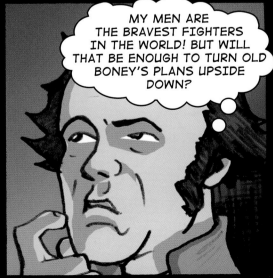

MY MEN ARE THE BRAVEST FIGHTERS IN THE WORLD! BUT WILL THAT BE ENOUGH TO TURN OLD BONEY'S PLANS UPSIDE DOWN?

Duke of Wellington

THE IRON DUKE

The Duke of Wellington was born Arthur Wellesley in 1769. His family was wealthy and powerful. He was educated at Eton, one of the most famous schools in England, and attended a military academy in France.

ENGLAND

Arthur Wellesley was a great soldier. He became famous for his victories against Napoleon in Portugal and Spain. In 1814, he was made the Duke of Wellington. He became known to his men as the "Iron Duke" because he was a stern man and a strict leader on the battlefield.

The Iron Duke was also known as Old Hookey (because of his nose) and Our Atty (Arthur). He was admired by his men, but not loved.

The Battle of Waterloo, in which he defeated Napoleon, was the Iron Duke's last battle. He went into politics and became Prime Minister of Britain in 1828. He died in 1852.

CHAPTER 4: THE BATTLE FOR WATERLOO!

SUNDAY, JUNE 18, 1815 – ONE OF THE MOST FAMOUS BATTLES IN HISTORY IS ABOUT TO TAKE PLACE! NAPOLEON SURVEYS THE FIELD FROM THE BACK OF HIS HORSE.

HIS CAVALRY FINDS THE MUD HARD TO MOVE THROUGH ...

... AND GUN CREWS STRAIN TO PULL CANNONS INTO POSITION.

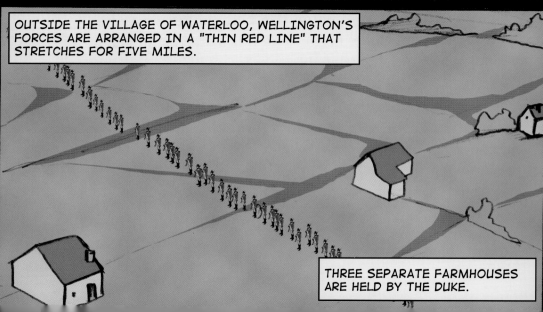

OUTSIDE THE VILLAGE OF WATERLOO, WELLINGTON'S FORCES ARE ARRANGED IN A "THIN RED LINE" THAT STRETCHES FOR FIVE MILES.

THREE SEPARATE FARMHOUSES ARE HELD BY THE DUKE.

NAPOLEON SENDS GENERAL GROUCHY AND 30,000 MEN TO FIND GENERAL BLUCHER AND HIS TROOPS.

BUT INSTEAD OF MOVING AWAY FROM THE FRENCH TROOPS, BLUCHER AND HIS MEN GO AROUND THEM!

THEY HEAD STRAIGHT FOR WELLINGTON TO JOIN THE BRITISH FORCES!

AGAIN AND AGAIN, NAPOLEON SENDS IN HIS TROOPS. THEY OVERRUN THE BRITISH CANNONS, DRIVING THE BRITISH TO TAKE COVER IN THE FARMHOUSES!

WHEN THE BRITISH COUNTERATTACK, THEY TURN THEIR CANNONS ON THE FRENCH!

THE IRON DUKE RIDES HIS HORSE UP AND DOWN THE THIN RED LINE, ENCOURAGING HIS MEN TO STAND FAST AND FIGHT!

BUT HIS MEN ARE BECOMING WEAKER. SOONER OR LATER, NAPOLEON WILL BREAK THROUGH!

THE IRON DUKE WONDERS WHERE BLUCHER AND HIS PRUSSIAN ARMY ARE.

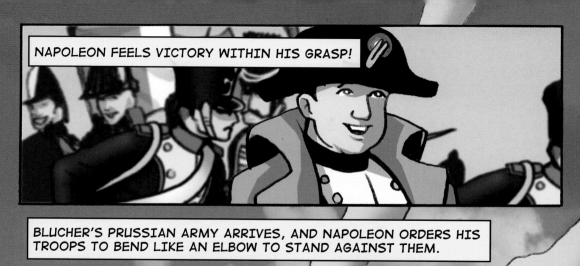

NAPOLEON FEELS VICTORY WITHIN HIS GRASP!

BLUCHER'S PRUSSIAN ARMY ARRIVES, AND NAPOLEON ORDERS HIS TROOPS TO BEND LIKE AN ELBOW TO STAND AGAINST THEM.

ACROSS THE FIELD, WELLINGTON IS PREPARING TO ORDER A RETREAT ...

... WHEN BLUCHER'S PRUSSIANS SMASH THROUGH NAPOLEON'S ARMY, AND SAVE THE DAY!

CHARGE!

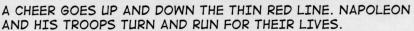

A CHEER GOES UP AND DOWN THE THIN RED LINE. NAPOLEON AND HIS TROOPS TURN AND RUN FOR THEIR LIVES.

HOORAY!

WELLINGTON AND BLUCHER HAVE WON THE BATTLE OF WATERLOO!

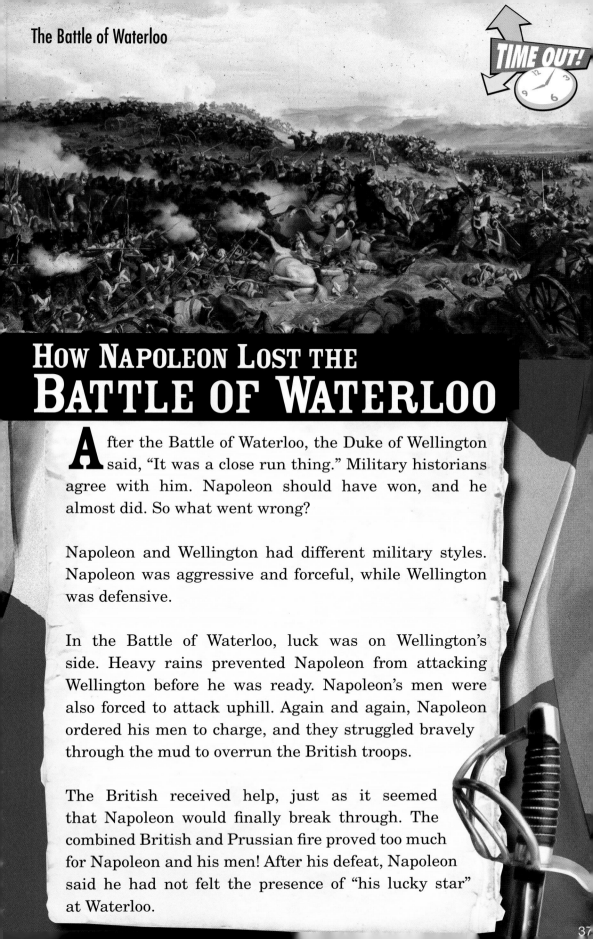

TIME OUT!

HOW NAPOLEON LOST THE
BATTLE OF WATERLOO

After the Battle of Waterloo, the Duke of Wellington said, "It was a close run thing." Military historians agree with him. Napoleon should have won, and he almost did. So what went wrong?

Napoleon and Wellington had different military styles. Napoleon was aggressive and forceful, while Wellington was defensive.

In the Battle of Waterloo, luck was on Wellington's side. Heavy rains prevented Napoleon from attacking Wellington before he was ready. Napoleon's men were also forced to attack uphill. Again and again, Napoleon ordered his men to charge, and they struggled bravely through the mud to overrun the British troops.

The British received help, just as it seemed that Napoleon would finally break through. The combined British and Prussian fire proved too much for Napoleon and his men! After his defeat, Napoleon said he had not felt the presence of "his lucky star" at Waterloo.

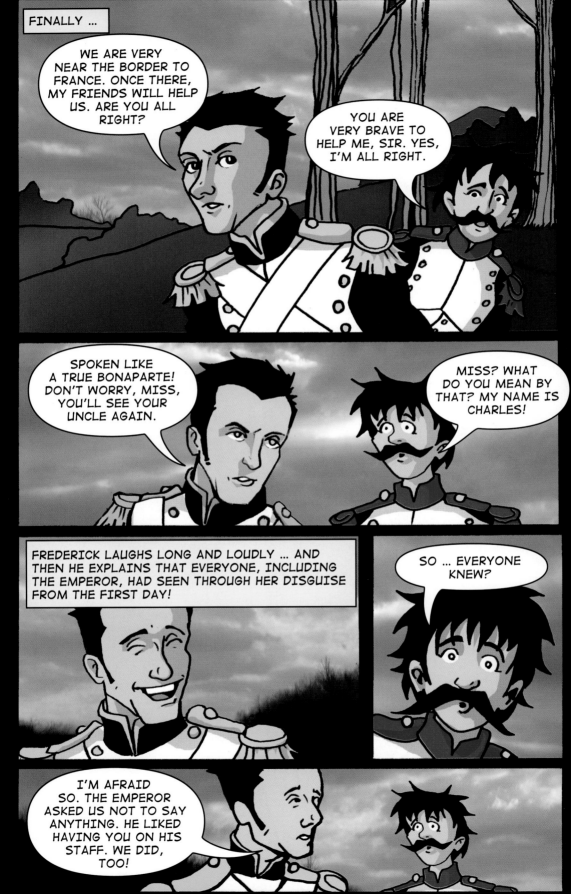

FIVE YEARS LATER. NOW 18, CHARLOTTE BONAPARTE MAKES THE 1,200-MILE JOURNEY FROM FRANCE TO ST. HELENA TO SEE HER BELOVED UNCLE NAPOLEON.

NO, UNCLE. I DIDN'T THINK IT WOULD WORK TWICE.

WE ALMOST WON AT WATERLOO! DON'T EVER FORGET THAT, MY DEAR. WE WERE UNLUCKY!

PAPA CALLS WATERLOO A GLORIOUS DEFEAT. PAPA SAYS YOU HAVE MADE THE NAME BONAPARTE FAMOUS FOREVER.

SO I HAVE, MY DEAR, SO I HAVE!

WHEN DID GREAT UNCLE NAPOLEON DIE, MAMA? WERE YOU THERE?

I WAS, LUCIEN. HE WAS VERY ILL WHEN I ARRIVED. AT THE END HE WAS VERY PEACEFUL.

CHARLOTTE SIGHS AS SHE REMEMBERS HER LAST VISIT WITH UNCLE NAPOLEON.

THE PEOPLE OF FRANCE WILL REMEMBER THEIR EMPEROR FOREVER!

The Tomb of Napoleon

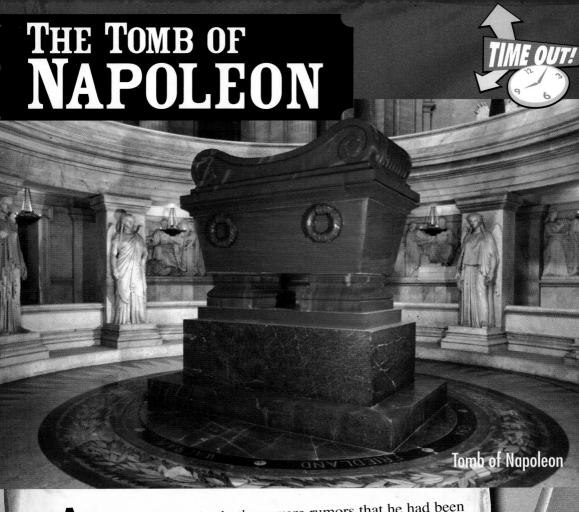

Tomb of Napoleon

After Napoleon's death, there were rumors that he had been poisoned. The cause of his death was never established for certain. Some historians believe that he died of arsenic poisoning from long exposure to the wallpaper glue used throughout his home on St. Helena.

Napoleon was first buried in St. Helena. In 1840, his remains were returned to France. On December 15, a funeral procession, marked by church bells and cannon fire, moved through the streets of Paris. A million people watched as the procession moved towards *Les Invalides*, a military installation that had also been a hospital for war veterans.

Napoleon rests in five coffins: one of tin, one of mahogany, two of lead, and one of ebony. They are arranged inside a massive block of stone brought from Finland. A circle below his tomb lists his military victories. *Les Invalides* today is a military museum and is visited by millions of people every year.

Crossing the Alps
— a painting by
Jacques-Louis David

LEGACY

Napoleon III

During his exile on St. Helena, Napoleon wrote his memoirs in which he explained how and why he fought his great battles.

The publication of his book two years after his death caused the French public to hope that his son, Napoleon II, might regain the throne. But Napoleon II died when he was 21 and never became Emperor. It was Napoleon's nephew, Louis Napoleon Bonaparte III, who became Emperor of France until 1870.

Today, many people admire Napoleon for his military genius and the far-reaching changes he introduced in law and government. Others criticize him for the deaths he caused in his military campaigns. Many French people died as a result of his wars.

Without a doubt, Napoleon was one of the greatest commanders in history. His ideas and actions dominated Europe completely. Today, we refer to the period he lived in as the Napoleonic Era.

INDEX